HEART & SOUL

GOSPEL SONGS...GOSPEL STYLE

ARRANGED BY CAMP KIRKLAND

ALLEGIS®
PUBLICATIONS
Kansas City, MO 64141

CONTENTS

We Shall See the King

Words and Music by
J. B. VAUGHN
Arranged by Camp Kirkland

With energy ♩ = ca. 84

CD: 1

Unison **mf**

There's a

bless - ed   time   that's com - ing,   com - ing   soon,   It

6

we shall see the King,_____ We shall see the King when__ He comes;__

He is com-ing in pow'r, we'll hail the bless-ed hour,__

We shall see the King when__ He comes._____

Unison

12

14

My Savior's Love

Words and Music by
CHARLES H. GABRIEL
Arranged by Camp Kirkland

*Trio may be SAT or STT (the high tenor singing the alto part as written)

Is my___ Sav - ior's love for me!

CD: 11

Unison **mf**

He

took my sins and my sor - rows; He made them His ver - y

CD: 13

20

22

I Go To Jesus

with

What a Friend We Have in Jesus

Words and Music by
DAN WHITTEMORE
Arranged by Camp Kirkland

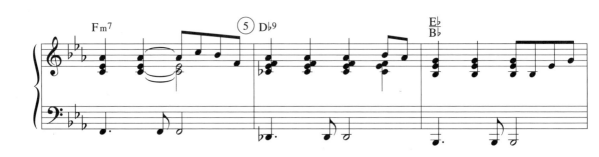

26

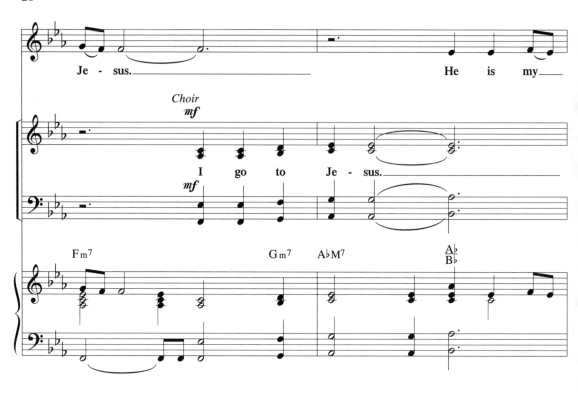

CD: 19

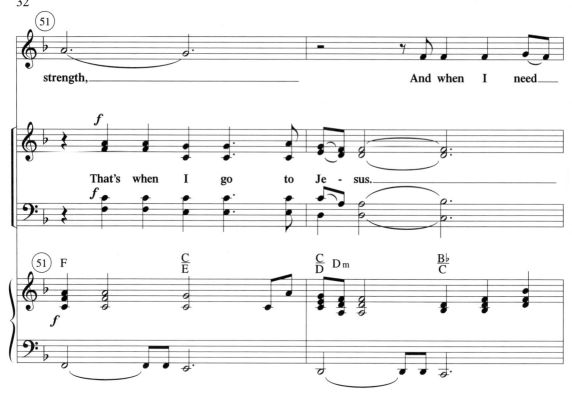

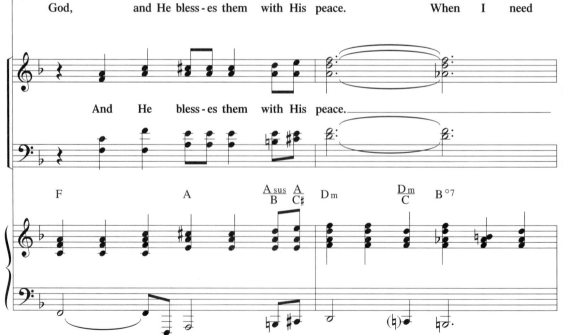

Children of God

with
We're Marching to Zion

Words and Music by
ANDERSON T. DAILEY
Arranged by Camp Kirkland

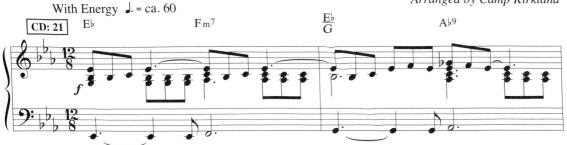

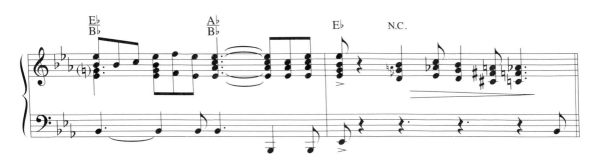

44

Jesus Is All the World to Me

Words and Music by
WILL L. THOMPSON
Arranged by Camp Kirkland

PLEASE NOTE: Copying of this product is not covered by CCLI licenses. For CCLI information call 1-800-234-2446.

50

52

53

54

55

I'm Climbing Up the Mountain

Words and Music by
MOSIE LISTER
Arranged by Camp Kirkland

CD: 33

66

68

We'll Understand It Better By and By

Words and Music by
C. A. TINDLEY
Arranged by Camp Kirkland

70

72

73

74

78

I Must Tell Jesus

Words and Music by
ELISHA A. HOFFMAN
Arranged by Camp Kirkland

I must tell Je - sus all of my tri - als; I can - not bear these

CD: 45

88

My Father Watches Over Me

W. C. MARTIN

CHARLES H. GABRIEL
Arranged by Camp Kirkland

90

92

94

95

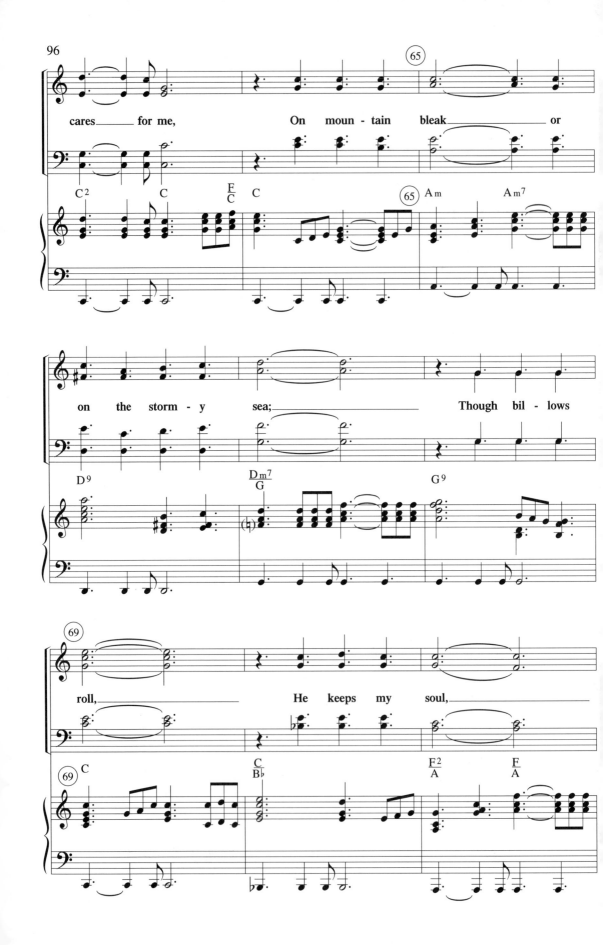

Revive Us Again

WILLIAM P. MACKAY

JOHN J. HUSBAND
Arranged by Camp Kirkland

104

108